PUFFIN BOOKS

THE Wimpy Kid
MOVIE DIARY

THE NEXT CHAPTER

OTHER BOOKS BY JEFF KINNEY

Diary of a Wimpy Kid

Diary of a Wimpy Kid: Rodrick Rules

Diary of a Wimpy Kid: The Last Straw

Diary of a Wimpy Kid: Dog Days

Diary of a Wimpy Kid: The Ugly Truth

Diary of a Wimpy Kid: Cabin Fever

Diary of a Wimpy Kid: The Third Wheel

Diary of a Wimpy Kid: Hard Luck

Diary of a Wimpy Kid: The Long Haul

Diary of a Wimpy Kid: Old School

Diary of a Wimpy Kid: Double Down

The Wimpy Kid Do-It-Yourself Book

The Wimpy Kid Movie Diary

COMING SOON: MORE *DIARY OF A WIMPY KID*

THE Wimpy Kid
MOVIE DIARY

THE NEXT CHAPTER

by Jeff Kinney

PUFFIN

PUFFIN BOOKS

UK | USA | Canada | Ireland | Australia
India | New Zealand | South Africa

Puffin Books is part of the Penguin Random House group of companies
whose addresses can be found at global.penguinrandomhouse.com.

www.penguin.co.uk   www.puffin.co.uk   www.ladybird.co.uk

First published in the USA by Amulet Books, an imprint of ABRAMS, 2017
Published in Great Britain by Puffin Books 2017

001

Film unit photography by Dan McFadden

Photos on pages 58, 60–62, 66, 74, 78 (bottom), 81, 84, 87, 88,
119 (middle), 128 (middle), 133 (bottom), 135 (top), 153,
164 (bottom), 165 (top), 173 (top), 178, and 179 copyright © 2017 David Bowers

Photo on page 198 (top) © 2017 Carol Tresan

Photos on pages 36, 37 (bottom), 38, 39, 46 (top), 59,
71 (bottom), 120, 124, 137, and 197 copyright © 2017 Jeff Kinney

Photos on pages 4, 5, and 190 used under license from iStockPhoto
Models on pages 42 and 113 used under license from iStockPhoto
Photograph on page 169 used under license
from Moviestore Collection Ltd/Alamy Stock Photos
Photograph on page 170 used under license from Photo 12/Alamy Stock Photos

Book and cover design by Jeff Kinney

Printed and bound in Italy

A CIP catalogue record for this book is available from the British Library

ISBN: 978-0-141-38819-9

All correspondence to
Puffin Books, Penguin Random House Children's
80 Strand, London WC2R ORL

MIX
Paper from
responsible sources
FSC
www.fsc.org   FSC® C018179

Penguin Random House is committed to a
sustainable future for our business, our readers
and our planet. This book is made from Forest
Stewardship Council® certified paper.

TO JASON

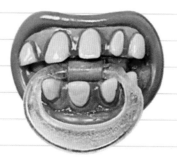

THE ROAD TO "THE LONG HAUL"

Making a movie is a lot like going on a road trip.
You start out with an idea of where you'd like to
go, you make plans, and eventually you head off on
your journey. There might be a few detours, and
there are bound to be a few bumps along the way.

But if everything goes as planned you'll end up
where you wanted to be, and you'll feel good about
your accomplishment. And, more often than not,
the trip will change you for the better.

This book is about the making of "Diary of a
Wimpy Kid: The Long Haul". Movie-making is full
of twists and turns, so there's a lot of ground to
cover. But every trip, and every story, starts at
the beginning.

1

A TRIP DOWN MEMORY LANE

Like many movies, "The Long Haul" was a book before it became a film. And, like many of the books in the Wimpy Kid series, this one was inspired by real-life events.

"The Long Haul" can trace its origins all the way back to the 1970s, when the Kinney family had a number of memorable, and awful, road trips.

Back in those days, the minivan hadn't been invented, so families tended to get around in station wagons, which weren't nearly as spacious.

If the Kinneys wanted to go somewhere far from home, they almost always drove. But a lot can go wrong on the road.

There was the time the Kinneys locked themselves out of the station wagon. Then there was the time one of the Kinney kids threw up in the backseat before they even got out of the driveway. And the time the Kinneys went camping in the mountains and had to sleep in the car when a bear invaded the campsite. That might sound hard to believe, but it really happened.

SNUFFLE
GRUNT

Two stories in particular became the inspiration for scenes in "The Long Haul". And both involve animals getting loose in the car.

3

The Kinney kids were raised in Maryland, where in the summertime it's common for a family to pick up a bushel of crabs at a roadside stand on the way home. That means driving with a paper bag full of live crabs.

One summer night, the car hit a pothole, and the paper bag tipped over. The crabs ran wild on the floor of the station wagon, and the terrified Kinney kids squealed in horror in the backseat.

Forty years later, that episode inspired the seagull scene in the book "The Long Haul". The details are all changed, but the idea is the same: it's terrifying to be trapped in a small space with panicked animals.

Another near-disaster occurred when the family's pet rabbit, Frisky, somehow got out of its cage in the back of the station wagon and tried to squirm through the back window.

But Mrs Kinney saved the day by leaping from the front seat to the back and grabbing the rabbit's hind legs before it had a chance to become roadkill.

Later on, this became the inspiration for a scene in "The Long Haul", when the pig gets out of its cooler and tries to escape.

Most families have at least one road-trip horror story just like these.

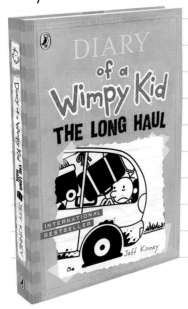

And that was the idea for "The Long Haul" — if Greg Heffley and his family went on a road trip across the country, what are all the things that could go wrong?

EASY AS ONE-TWO-THREE

In 2015, there were ten Wimpy Kid books, and three of them had already been made into movies.

"The Long Haul" was the first Wimpy Kid book that was actually written with a movie in mind. And the timing was perfect: the studio had started to think about making a new Wimpy Kid movie.

Everyone agreed, "The Long Haul" was a great idea for the next film. The first three movies were set in the Heffleys' town, but this was a chance to get Greg and his family out of their regular world and on the road.

But the movie would have to be different from the book. If you've ever seen a movie that's based on a book you've read, you've probably noticed that there are a lot of changes. That's because if you film a book exactly the way it's written, chances are it won't make a very good movie.

Even though every movie is different, audiences expect certain things to happen when they're watching a film. Almost all movies are written in three sections called "acts". Let's take a look at what happens in each act, using one of Greg and Rowley's movies as an example.

ACT ONE

We meet the main character, or "hero".

We learn about the hero's world and the problems the hero faces.

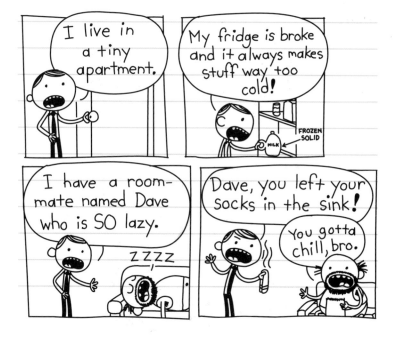

Something unexpected happens.

The hero is faced with a big decision.

ACT TWO

The hero takes action!

In the middle of Act Two, something serious happens.

Things get harder and harder for the hero, and the hero hits rock bottom.

ACT THREE

The hero figures out a solution to the problems and starts to "win".

Something unexpected happens, and things are worse than ever for the hero.

The hero remembers the lessons from what's happened before and finds a new solution.

The hero uses those lessons and (usually) wins!

Believe it or not, almost every movie you'll see follows the same beats of a three-act structure. "The Wizard of Oz", "Star Wars", and every superhero movie that's ever been made —if you really think about it, they're all the same basic story.

The next time you watch a movie, keep track of the beats. Try to figure out where one act ends and the next act begins. And once you can do all that, you'll be able to guess what will happen next in the story.

But be careful. It might not make you popular.

GOING AROUND IN CIRCLES

Just because the rules for writing a script are pretty simple, that doesn't mean it's easy for a screenwriter to get everything right the first time around. For most movies, there are at least a dozen drafts, and it takes months of rewriting to get a script right.

The film-makers knew that certain changes had to be made to "The Long Haul" to make the story work as a movie. In the book, the family sets out on a road trip, but they're not really trying to get anywhere. They just drive around for a few days and end up where they started, back at home.

But that wouldn't really work for a movie. It's important for the audience to have something to root for, so the screenwriters gave the Heffleys a goal: to reach Meemaw's house in time for her ninetieth birthday party.

Meemaw is Greg's great grandmother, and she made an appearance in Book 8, "Hard Luck".

In a movie, it's important to have a "ticking clock". When there's something that has to happen by a certain time, it makes everything seem more urgent—and keeps the audience on the edge of their seats.

Would the Heffleys get to Meemaw's in time for the party? Or would Greg screw everything up and make them miss it? That's the question at the centre of this movie.

The idea for Meemaw's birthday party stuck and made it into the final script. But there were lots of other ideas that didn't make the cut.

Here are some scenes that were part of the "Long Haul" script at one time, but were later thrown out.

Greg, Fregley and Chirag have an epic laser-tag fight at a bowling alley.

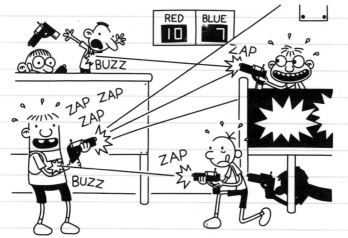

Greg's family is rescued by a Spanish-speaking heavy metal group called Metallichihuahua.

Greg and Rodrick are chased by a charging bull at the country fair.

The Heffleys and the Beardos get into a tug-of-war over a lounge chair at a water park.

As you can see, not every idea is a winner. But trying out lots of different ideas can help point you in the right direction.

A FRESH START

Audiences loved the actors who played the characters in the first three films, especially Zach Gordon, who played Greg Heffley, and Robert Capron, who played Greg's best friend, Rowley Jefferson.

But by the time "The Long Haul" was in development, Zach and Robert had grown up to be young men and were headed off to college. So there was no chance they'd be returning to their roles as middle-schoolers.

The great thing about cartoon characters is that no matter how many years go by, they never change. It's too bad it's not the same way with actors!

GREG
2007

GREG
2017

While the script was being developed, the film-makers started their search for a new Greg and Rowley. A casting announcement was made inviting kids to try out for the roles.

CASTING

DIARY
of a
Wimpy Kid

INTERNATIONAL
BESTSELLER

THE LONG HAUL

Jeff Kinney

Casting for the role of: Greg Heffley and Rowley Jefferson in the 20th Century Fox movie based upon the best selling Diary of Wimpy Kid series by Jeff Kinney.

Two thousand boys auditioned for each character. Some were experienced actors, and some were stepping in front of the camera for the first time.

When actors try out for a part in a movie, television show or commercial, chances are that they won't get it. Most of the time, it's not because of a lack of talent —it's just that there's someone else who's a better fit for the role.

Rejection can be hard to take, especially for a kid. But anyone who wants to be an actor has to get used to dealing with disappointment, and to be ready the next time a great role comes up. It's all part of being a professional.

When you're trying out for a role, it's not so
important how you look —it's important that you
can capture the SPIRIT of the character you're
trying out for.

The role of Greg Heffley is tricky to cast. Greg
is a kid who's always looking out for himself, and
he does some things that aren't so admirable. But
audiences need to LIKE Greg, or they won't root
for him. And if the audience isn't rooting for
Greg, then the movie won't work.

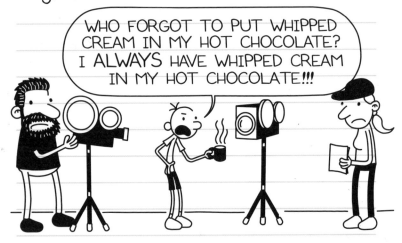

It took months to find the right Greg. In the
end, the film-makers chose Jason Drucker, a young
actor who had appeared in a handful of TV shows.

Everyone who saw Jason's audition tape knew he could pull off the role and get audiences to cheer him on.

With his long, curly hair, Jason didn't LOOK much like Greg Heffley. But that could always be fixed later.

Greg's best friend, Rowley Jefferson, is the opposite of Greg in many ways. He's innocent, kind and loyal, and is a happy-go-lucky kid.

No one captured the essence of Rowley better
than a young actor named Owen Asztalos, who had
appeared in a few television shows and commercials
before auditioning for "The Long Haul".

But before the film-makers could sign off on the
two young actors, they needed to see if the boys
had "chemistry".

In movies, chemistry is the connection that two
people have when they're together on-screen.
Sometimes, you can have two talented actors,
but for some reason they don't connect when the
cameras roll. And if your co-stars don't have good
chemistry, the audience will sense it.

Fortunately, when the director had the two boys do a test scene, something clicked between them. The pair made a believable Greg and Rowley.

The actors went home not knowing if they had got the roles. A few weeks later, the director called both boys to tell them the good news: they'd be starring in the new movie as Greg and Rowley. Jason and Owen couldn't have been more excited.

The two actors were each at the start of a whole new journey, and their lives were about to change. Both boys were eager to discover just where the road might take them.

CALLING ALL HEFFLEYS

Not only was Greg recast for the new movie but new actors were picked to play the rest of the Heffleys as well.

Alicia Silverstone was chosen to play Greg's mom, Susan. Alicia has had lots of memorable roles in films, television shows and music videos. Once, she even played Batgirl in a Batman movie. In addition to being 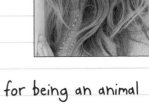 an actress, Alicia is famous for being an animal rights activist.

Tom Everett Scott was picked to play Greg's dad, Frank. Tom has appeared in lots of films as well, and coincidentally his first starring role was alongside his good friend Steve Zahn, who played Greg's dad in the first three Wimpy Kid movies.

The role of Greg's teenage older brother, Rodrick, went to Charlie Wright, an actor whose movie career was starting to take off. Charlie came to his audition dressed in the type of outfit Rodrick might wear, which helped him get the part.

The most challenging role to fill was Greg's younger brother, Manny, because the character would be played not by one actor —but two.

When a movie calls for very young children to play important roles, film-makers usually cast twins. That way, if one of the kids is being uncooperative (or just needs to take a nap), the sibling can be swapped in.

The kids playing Manny couldn't be too young, or they wouldn't be able to remember their lines.

But they couldn't be too old, either, or they'd outgrow the part if there were future films.

The role went to Dylan and Wyatt Walters, a pair of three-year-old boys. But Dylan and Wyatt aren't twins, they're triplets — they have a sister as well. Dylan and Wyatt had never been on camera before, so making a movie would be a whole new experience for them.

The actors lived in different areas of the country, but soon they'd all be headed to the same place, coming together as the Heffleys.

LOCATION, LOCATION

One of the biggest decisions the film-makers had to make was where to shoot "The Long Haul". The first three Wimpy Kid movies were shot in Vancouver, Canada. But since the new film was about a family's road trip through the United States, it really had to be filmed there.

It wouldn't be practical to shoot a movie that covered the kind of distance the Heffleys were travelling, though. A film like "The Long Haul" requires a cast and crew of hundreds of people, along with all the equipment they use to get their jobs done. And it's just too expensive to move all that gear around every day.

The film-makers needed to find an area in the United States that had a wide range of scenery. That way, they could make it LOOK like the Heffleys were travelling a great distance, even though all the scenes would be filmed close to one another.

They decided on Georgia, a beautiful state in the southern U.S. with a diverse landscape.

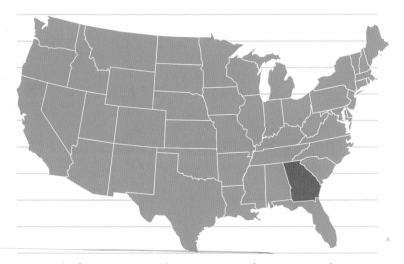

One of the reasons Georgia was chosen was because its capital is Atlanta. Many television shows and films are made in that city, so there are lots of talented people who live and work in the area.

In fact, some of today's biggest blockbusters are shot in Atlanta, including many of the big superhero movies.

Once Atlanta was chosen as "home base" for the film, the director and a small team of location scouts spent weeks driving all over the area, looking for the perfect places to capture the scenes described in the screenplay. They took pictures and video of each location they visited.

SNAP

Scouting is hard work, but it's an important step in making a good movie. On the following pages are a handful of spots that were chosen for the film, and the scenes in the "Long Haul" book that they match up with.

SETTING IT IN MOTION

With the final details of the script getting nailed down, it was time to get serious about making this movie. There's a ton of work that needs to be done before the actors arrive and filming starts, and this phase is called "pre-production".

A team of artists, set designers, wardrobe specialists, prop masters and others set up shop in an old elementary school in Atlanta.

Each team took over an empty classroom to start doing their work.

If you walked through the hallways of the school during pre-production for "The Long Haul", you'd see a lot of crazy stuff going on. In one room, you'd find the prop master painting lips on a dummy with bad teeth.

A few feet away, you'd find an illustrator making up a "Mommy Meal" bag in the same handwriting as Mrs Heffley.

Nearby you'd see piles of luggage to fill the Heffleys' boat, an assortment of car seats and plastic potties for Manny to sit on, and various cardboard signs with Rodrick's handwriting on them.

On a cluttered table, you'd find a tube of cinnamon rolls and packets of icing.

Out in the hallway, you'd come across the assistant prop master painting a pair of underwear with glue to make it stiff as a board so it could be flung like a Frisbee.

An arm's length away, you'd see someone mixing a giant vat of fake mud to splatter on the actors during filming.

And just outside the doorway you'd see mannequins dressed in the Heffleys' clothes to test how the mud would look when it was splattered on the actors.

Down the hallway, you'd find a ton of activity in a room marked "Art Department". This team's job is to design everything you see on-screen that doesn't already exist, from small props to giant movie sets.

The art department taped pictures of the illustrations from "The Long Haul" to the walls so they could stay as true to the original drawings as possible. On the following pages are some of the designs created by the art department, along with the illustrations that inspired them.

CINNAMON ROLLS

with Icing

8 Cinnamon Rolls
KEEP REFRIGERATED

HEAT • MAKE • EAT!

1. HEAT Oven to 400. Grease round cake pan.	**3. BAKE** 13 to 17 minutes or until golden brown
2. PLACE rolls in pan, cinnamon topping up	**4. SPREAD** with icing!

Nutrition Facts

CINNAMON ROLLS

PAPA PEPE'S

PAPA PEPE'S
PEPPERONI PIZZA

NET WT 14.25 OZ (403

42

Looking at some of these images, you're probably wondering why the designers went to the trouble of putting so much detail into each design. Does the package of cinnamon rolls really need to have a list of nutrition facts, plus step-by-step cooking instructions? Does the microwave pizza box need to have the words "Cook thoroughly, enjoy wholeheartedly" written in itsy-bitsy print?

The short answer is "yes". The art department's job is to make the world of the movie as complete as possible. This helps the actors do their jobs, because if their world is believable it's easier for them to pretend they're really in it.

Besides, the designers take a lot of pride in the work they do. Even if every detail doesn't show up on-screen, they can feel good about a job well done.

IT'S A SIGN

Any time you go on a road trip, you're bound to see lots of interesting signs along the way. Here are some of the signs the art department created to bring the Heffleys' journey to life.

44

All the signs for the movie were first created on a computer screen, and later made out of materials such as metal, plastic, glass and wood. The signs were then "weathered" to make them look like they'd been outside for a while. It's all part of creating a realistic world for the movie.

But not everything is as it seems. The L'il Critters Petting Zoo sign looks like it's made out of iron, but it's really made out of plastic that's painted to look rusty.

The effect is so convincing that when you touch the sign you're expecting it to be heavy. But it's actually as light as a feather.

Weathering signs is a real art form. Check out the difference between the digital design of this sign and the version that's seen in the film.

In the movie, the Heffleys stay at a handful of hotels and motels, and each one has a sign that reflects its unique character.

One of the motels is called "The Laughing Pines", and it has a large sign illuminated with neon lights. The sign weighed hundreds of pounds and took several weeks to create but is only seen for about three seconds on-screen.

COME EAR OFTEN?

One of the biggest undertakings for the art department was to create a family-style restaurant called Corny's. If you're a fan of the Wimpy Kid books, you might remember Corny's from "The Third Wheel".

Corny's was in the first scene of the movie, so creating the set began long before filming started. It was an ambitious project, because there are lots of elements to a restaurant: signage, menus, plates, napkins, furniture, merchandise...they all needed to be designed and created.

No detail was overlooked. The designers even made buttons for the Corny's staff to wear.

All the signage in the restaurant reflected the unique character of the place.

CORNY'S BILL O' RIGHTS

YOU'VE GOT THE RIGHT TO...
EAT LIBERALLY

YOU'VE GOT THE RIGHT TO...
HAVE DESSERT FIRST

YOU'VE GOT THE RIGHT TO...
EAT MORE FOR LESS

YOU'VE GOT THE RIGHT TO HAVE...
QUALITY FAMILY TIME

YOU'VE GOT THE RIGHT TO...
CHOOSE FREELY

It's possible the designers got a little TOO carried away. They even created a backstory about the first-ever Corny's restaurant and its original cook, Ron Hammond.

The images are never actually seen in the movie, but now they're part of the Wimpy Kid universe forever.

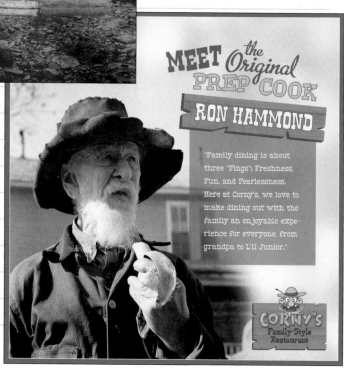

MEET *the Original* PREP COOK
RON HAMMOND

"Family dining is about three "Fings": Freshness, Fun, and Fearlessness. Here at Corny's, we love to make dining out with the family an enjoyable experience for everyone, from grandpa to L'il Junior."

CORNY'S
Family-Style Restaurant

While the artists were creating all the great stuff to go inside Corny's, the scouting team was searching for the perfect spot to set up the imaginary restaurant.

They found an empty building outside Atlanta that had recently been an Asian seafood restaurant, and they thought it could be a perfect fit.

But before the art department started doing the real work to transform the building into Corny's, they did some mock-ups on the computer to see what things would look like. In the design world, this is called creating a "composite". Here are some shots of the empty restaurant and the Cornified composites.

Once everyone agreed that the designs looked good, work started on getting the restaurant ready for filming. Slowly but surely, the interior of the building was transformed into a brightly coloured family-style restaurant.

On top of dressing up the restaurant with signs, new tables and chairs, and new carpeting, a colourful play structure was brought in.

The script called for a ball pit, so a crew had to bring in heavy machinery to dig a square hole in the floor, which would later be filled with plastic balls.

Work began transforming the outside of the building as well. The wood trim was given a new paint job in a Corny's colour scheme, and an illuminated sign was hung above the doorway.

The building was on a busy stretch of road and, when the Corny's sign went up, some people came by to check out the joint and maybe have a bite to eat.

If your movie set looks good enough to convince the public it's a real restaurant, that's the sign of good work. Aaron Osborne and his team of designers had passed their first big test and were ready for the start of filming.

Corny himself would be proud.

THIS LITTLE PIGGY

As the start of filming approached, everyone was a little nervous about one thing: the pig. In the book, the pig plays a major role, and there was no question it would be in the film.

The first task was to choose which KIND of pig would be in the film. There are all sorts of pigs out there, and the film-makers had to pick the breed that would be the best fit for the movie.

A husband-and-wife team who trained animals to work in films came in to discuss the pros and cons of each type of pig. They even brought a few pigs with them for show-and-tell.

The film-makers enjoyed having some time with the baby pigs, and it was a fun day to be in the movie business.

Everyone loved the adorable baby Yorkshire piglets, which were the type of pig used in the movie "Babe". But the problem with that breed is that they grow up fast, and the full-grown version isn't as cuddly as the little version.

During a two-month shoot, a Yorkshire pig wouldn't reach its adult size, but the growth would be noticeable to audiences.

The film-makers needed a type of pig that was cute, smart and didn't grow too big or too fast. The breed that checked all those boxes was the Juliana variety.

Juliana pigs are an intelligent, playful and affectionate breed — perfect qualities for the Heffleys' new pet. Most important, they stay on the small side, even as adults.

But just as the film-makers needed a backup Manny, they needed a backup pig. Two young pigs that were the same age were picked for the part and brought to the production offices to audition.

They seemed perfect for the role, but what really sealed the deal was when they sat in Manny's plastic potty.

Once the pigs were chosen, a special effects artist came in to sculpt a replica in clay. But the reason for that is a story for a little later on.

NOW, ABOUT THAT HAIR...

A few weeks before filming was set to begin, a number of the actors came to the production offices to participate in a read-through of the script, try on their costumes and meet with the director.

But a big reason for the trip was to get the actors' hair right for the movie. The film-makers thought it was best to have Jason's and Owen's hair more or less match the

hairstyles of Zach Gordon and Robert Capron in the first three films.

Jason Drucker's long hair had already been cut short when he did a test screening with Owen.

But Jason's hair is naturally curly, and it had to be constantly straightened so it didn't get out of control.

Owen normally wore his hair parted to the side, but now it was time to transform him into Rowley, who has more of a bowl cut in the films.

Things weren't as straightforward with Charlie, who was set to play Rodrick. Charlie likes to wear his hair long, which doesn't really match Rodrick's spiky hair in the books.

But Charlie's long hair looked good for a rock-and-roll drummer, so he got to keep his look. It was more important to capture the spirit of the characters than their exact appearance.

Alicia and Tom got to keep their normal hairstyles, too. And that was probably a relief to both of them, because their cartoon counterparts didn't exactly have the coolest hair.

ACTION!

In mid-September, everyone came together
for the start of filming. There was a lot of
excitement the first day on set, and the actors
and crew were eager to get started.

Corny's was ready for its big day. The tables

were set and
the place was
looking spiffy.
But a restaurant
isn't really a
restaurant
without food.

Before filming started, chefs made food—piles and piles of it. In the book, the all-you-can-eat buffet is Corny's most popular feature, so there needed to be heaps of food of every variety.

After all, Corny wants to make sure everyone who visits his restaurant gets their fill.

Filming at Corny's was scheduled to last four days. That created some challenges, because the food on the tables needed to look fresh, day after day.

You've probably noticed that when food's left out it starts to go bad. So the cooks were constantly making new food to replace what was on the tables.

The drinks were a different matter. The challenge there was the ice. If real ice was used, it would melt under the hot lights. So the prop department filled the drinks with plastic ice cubes instead.

Usually, movies don't shoot in order. But for "The Long Haul", the opening scenes were actually the first ones to be filmed. So, when the Heffley family arrives at Corny's restaurant, it was the first time the actors were sharing a scene together.

They got to know one another—and Rowley—by chatting at their table in Children's Alley.

But they wouldn't be the only ones getting to know one another that day. In the book, Corny's is absolutely packed with people.

The movie would be the same way. Dozens of people signed up to be extras for the scenes at Corny's, and when they arrived they were seated together as families for the film.

They'd spend the next few days sitting at their tables and bonding over their shared experience.

Being an extra is hard work. The hours are long, and there's a lot of waiting around. Sometimes your moment on camera gets cut, and you don't even end up in the final film.

That was the case with the Corny's mascot, who had to put on an uncomfortable costume and wear make-up every day on set. Even though he got cut from the movie, at least he made this book!

One of the last scenes to film at Corny's was the hardest to pull off. It was a single shot all the way through the restaurant, starting on a crying baby's face, weaving through the buffet area and ending up at the feet of the Heffley family.

This is what film-makers call a long tracking shot. Everyone in the scene has to do everything exactly right, or it will ruin the take and they'll have to do it all over again.

In a restaurant filled with extras and a lot of food and drinks, there are tons of things that can go wrong.

The first few takes of the scene didn't go as planned, which was stressful because time was running out to get the shot right. But for the very last one things went perfectly. To celebrate, the cinematographer and director treated themselves to ice cream from the soft-serve machine.

As filming wrapped up on the Corny's set, the production team got ready to say goodbye to the restaurant they had created.

They put together a time capsule filled with cool stuff, like the film's script, menus, Corny's merchandise and a note for whoever might find it in the future. Then they put the time capsule into the ball pit, which was later filled with concrete.

Who knows? In a few hundred years, maybe some of our descendants will uncover the time capsule. And they'll probably wonder why plastic ice cubes were used in our drinks.

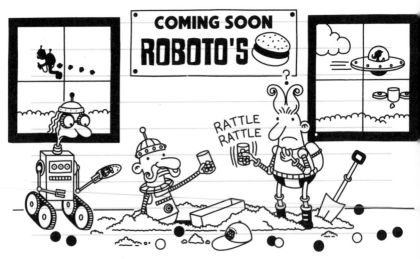

MIDDLE OF THE ROAD

After filming in one place for a few days, it was time to hit the road and start filming scenes of the Heffleys travelling. This was the first chance to take the van—and boat—out for a spin.

But the van isn't always what it seems. Sometimes it's an ordinary vehicle that a typical family would drive. At other times it's a special vehicle called a "buck car" that's designed for movie-making.

The buck car sits on a pair of rails and breaks apart in pieces.

When a piece of the van needs to be moved, it just slides out of the way. This allows the director to get shots of the interior of the

vehicle that would be much more difficult to get in an ordinary van.

The buck car came in handy lots of different times during the filming of "The Long Haul". For some shots it was convenient to use, but other shots would've been nearly impossible to film without it.

When you're shooting on a public road, you have to close it off to make sure nobody drives on to the movie set. And for a film like "The Long Haul", there are plenty of good reasons for that.

The cars you see going by in the background of a film are actually being driven by stunt drivers.

And if the cars aren't going anywhere, chances are there are extras at the wheels.

It's easy to film when the vehicles are standing still. But things get a lot more complicated when the cars are moving.

A special truck is used to film vehicles while rolling. The flatbed in the back is designed to hold the cameras, the director and a few other key people. The truck is followed by a caravan of vehicles that carry the rest of the team.

The vehicles are spray-painted completely black so that they don't cast a reflection in the windows of passing cars.

That's especially important when shooting a close-up like this one.

The more action there is in a scene, the more challenging it is to film. The most complex road scene in the movie is when Greg's father takes a work call, and chaos breaks out inside the van. The whole scene went off without a hitch, and no people, or pigs, were harmed in the process.

A STICKY SITUATION

The script for "The Long Haul" called for the Heffley family to get really messy on their journey to Meemaw's. Mud, bird poop, feathers, toiletries, cinnamon-bun goo —you name it, and the Heffleys were covered in it.

Most of the time, it's the hair and make-up department's job to make actors look good on-screen. But for "The Long Haul", more often than not they needed to look BAD.

The actors playing the Heffleys weren't the ONLY ones who had to get messy, though.

In most films, lighting doubles or stand-ins are used so that the film-makers can get everything set up just right before the real actors are brought in. For "The Long Haul", each member of the Heffley family had a double who was the same height. And like the actors who played the Heffleys, the stand-ins enjoyed getting to know one another during filming.

Everything the actors who played the Heffley family went through in the film, the lighting doubles had to go through, too. And they had to go through it FIRST.

So every time Greg and his family were sprayed with shampoo, attacked by seagulls, or splattered with mud, remember that they weren't the only ones who had to suffer.

In one of the first messy scenes that was filmed, the Beardo family's van runs over a bag of toiletries, which explodes and covers the Heffleys in a mix of shampoo, conditioner and make-up. The film-makers tried different combinations of liquids in different colours and amounts until they got the mixture just right.

Then the liquid was loaded into air-powered cannons that were designed to safely splatter people.

When the effect looked right, the actors playing the Heffleys were brought in for their turn in front of the cameras.

Everyone seemed to be a good sport about getting covered in slop, but some days were tougher than others. Usually everyone could get cleaned up right after their messy moment, but sometimes that wasn't possible.

At one point in the film, the Heffleys get covered head to toe in mud.

It wasn't REAL mud, thankfully — it was actually a mixture of cornstarch and food colouring. But, still, nobody found it pleasant to be caked in it.

Of course, the actors could take showers at night, but during filming it was all mud, all the time. And you really couldn't blame anyone if they got a little grouchy.

ANI-MANNY AND ROBO-PIG

One of the big questions at the start of filming was how the twins playing Manny would behave once the cameras were rolling. Movie-making is time-consuming, hard work, and there was no telling how Dylan and Wyatt would feel about it.

In the first three movies, Manny appeared in just a handful of scenes. But in "The Long Haul", Manny would need to be in almost every single shot. So the film-makers had to come up with some creative solutions to make sure everything went smoothly on set.

One of the simplest solutions was the dummy that Manny has in his mouth for a big chunk of the movie.

The film-makers knew from experience that toddlers can be chatty when other actors are saying their lines. So giving the actors who played Manny a dummy was a simple way to keep them occupied.

The other solutions were a little more complex. For parts of the movie, Manny is sitting in his car seat, and sometimes he's napping. The film-makers decided to put a realistic mannequin in place of the twins for the scenes where Manny was asleep.

But this was no ordinary doll. Inside the mannequin were complex robotics that allowed "Manny" to suck on his dummy, turn his head to the side, and even kick his legs in his sleep.

This would help
create the illusion
that Manny was
really "alive", even
if he was napping.
Manny's movements
were controlled by
a special effects
technician standing a
few feet offscreen.

The "Ani-Manny", as
it came to be called
by the crew, was so convincing that when people
came across it on set, they thought it was a real

human being.
Even Dylan
and Wyatt
seemed a
little confused
when they
first saw it.

Manny wasn't the only one who got the robotic treatment. An animatronic version of the pig was created as well. That was the purpose of the clay model from the pre-production phase.

Animals can be difficult to work with, and there was no telling what a live pig might do when the cameras were rolling. So the film-makers decided to use a live, trained pig most of the time, and then use a remote-controlled robot in special situations.

Juliana pigs don't love to be held, but in two of the scenes the script called for Manny to cradle the pig in his arms.

For those scenes, the animatronic pig needed to be convincing enough in its close-ups that moviegoers wouldn't notice it wasn't a real animal.

The robot pig could do it all —blink, wag its tail, wiggle its rear end, and open and close its mouth. It really was a marvel of technology.

The animatronic pig had its big moment on the day Manny and his pet reunite at the L'il Critters Petting Zoo, which is a scene that happens at the end of the "Long Haul" book but was filmed early on for the movie.

For the first part of the scene, the real-life Manny and the real-life pig sprint towards each other.

One of the pig's trainers used snacks to get it to run towards the camera.

When Manny and the pig come together, Manny holds the pig in his arms as it wags its tail with joy. By then, the real pig had been swapped out for the animatronic one. And the whole scene is so convincing no one would hold it against you for getting a little misty-eyed.

WINGING IT

One of the most memorable scenes in the book is when a flock of seagulls invades the Heffleys' van to gobble up Greg's Cheez Curlz.

Of all the scenes in the movie, this was the one that most closely matched what happens in the book. The director planned all the action in advance with rough drawings, and then a storyboard artist, Dawud Anyabwile, sketched out each scene.

There's an amazing level of artistry and detail that goes into planning a scene like this one.

Feeling miserable, Greg reaches for a bag of Cheez Curlz to comfort-eat.

A SEAGULL lands on the edge of the broken sunroof and looks in. It's kinda cute.

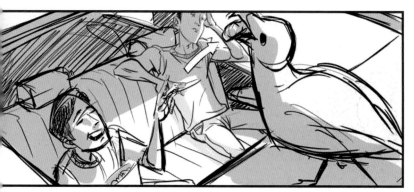

Greg shows it his bag of Cheez Curlz. The seagull cocks its head. Greg tosses up a Cheez Curl. The seagull catches it and looks to Greg for more.

Susan: Oh Greg, I wouldn't encourage them.

Greg: There's only one.

But when Greg looks up …

… there are TWO seagulls.

Greg tosses them another.

Frank: Seriously, Greg, that's enough.

Greg looks up again and the sunroof is surrounded by seagulls. This is creepy.

Greg: Yeah. Er, guys, can you close the sunroof?

Frank: Rodrick gummed it up, remember?

Zoom in on seagull.

Close up on Greg's face.

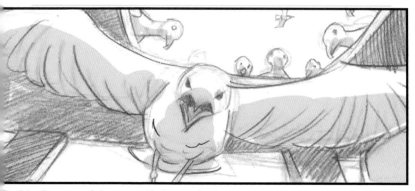

Suddenly, one of the seagulls jumps in the car and grabs Greg's bag of
Cheez Curlz.

Greg tries to hold on to the bag.

The seagull flies away with the bag ...

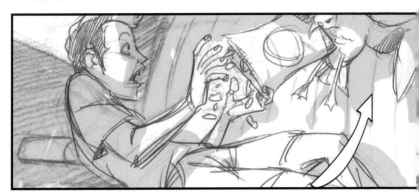

... spilling Cheez Curlz into the van as it flies away.

'he Heffleys are covered with Cheez Curlz.

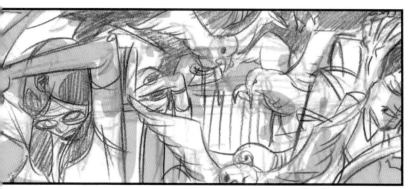

reedy seagulls swarm in through the sunroof. Everybody screams.

'rank panics …

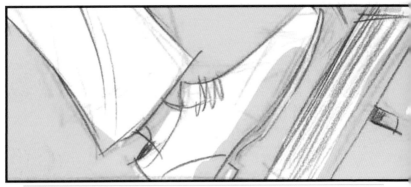

… and accidentally stomps on the gas pedal.

The minivan full of seagulls accelerates a few feet …

.. then rolls down a grassy median ...

.. slamming into the bottom, and then finally coming to a stop.

The doors burst open and the seagulls swarm out ...

...followed by the Heffleys. They are freaked out, roughed up, and covered in feathers and poop.

Greg breathes a sigh of relief ...

... until one last seagull swoops in ...

. . and grabs a Cheez Curl from his hair.

The minivan hisses as smoke exhales from under the hood.

Everyone looks at Greg like everything is his fault, again.

If you thought real birds —or animatronic ones — were used for this scene, you'd be mistaken. The seagulls in the movie were all created on computers. And when it came time to film on set the digital seagulls hadn't even been created yet.

So, without any real birds to react to, the actors had to do what they do best —make believe.

The cast had to pretend the seagulls were in the car, and a few of the crew members had to pretend to be seagulls. Here's what it looked like on set when the seagulls drop the contents of the Cheez Curlz bag into the Heffleys' van.

And here's the assistant director using a seagull cutout to pluck the last Cheez Curl out of Greg's hair.

Months after filming ended, a special effects team got to work, digitally adding seagulls to the shots. The renderings started off rough, then got better with each pass.

Here are a few shots of each stage in the process, starting with the way things looked during filming, and at each step along the way. See if you can match the shots with the storyboard drawings on the previous pages.

In the early days of film-making, special effects were very basic.

But as special effects have got better, audiences have become more and more demanding that everything they see on-screen looks "real".

The seagulls in "The Long Haul" look great by today's standards. But thirty years from now audiences may see them very differently.

THE ONLY GAME IN TOWN

One of the biggest set pieces in the movie is for a scene that's not in the book. In the film, the family is headed to Meemaw's party, but Greg has other plans. He secretly reroutes the GPS to take him to Player Expo, a huge gathering of game enthusiasts.

For Greg, Player Expo is like heaven. He needs to figure out a way to get there, no matter what.

To film the scenes for Player Expo, the film-makers rented out the Georgia International Convention Centre. Months before they got there, the art department planned out every inch of the convention hall.

They made a three-dimensional miniature paper model of every booth that would fill out the convention centre. The model also helped the director plan out his shots.

Creating Player Expo was a huge undertaking, because the giant hall needed to be packed with video-game booths, walls of monitors and lots of other eye candy for moviegoers to enjoy.

Player Expo would be filled with real products as well as ones that were made up. The design team had a blast creating concepts for games that weren't actually real but probably should be.

Here are some of the games that exist only in the Wimpy Kid movie universe...for now.

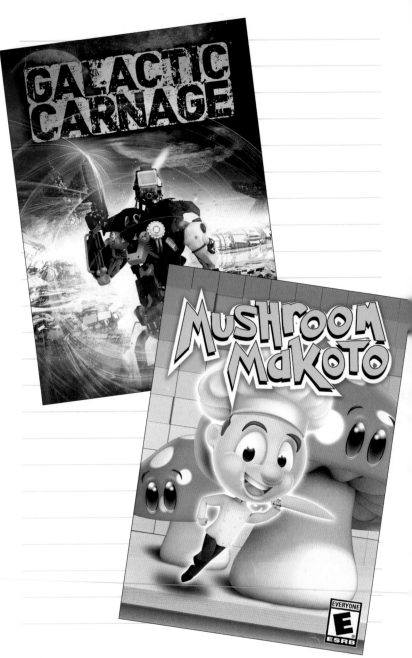

114

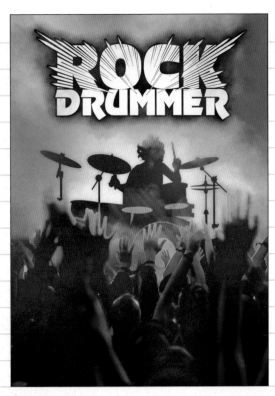

116

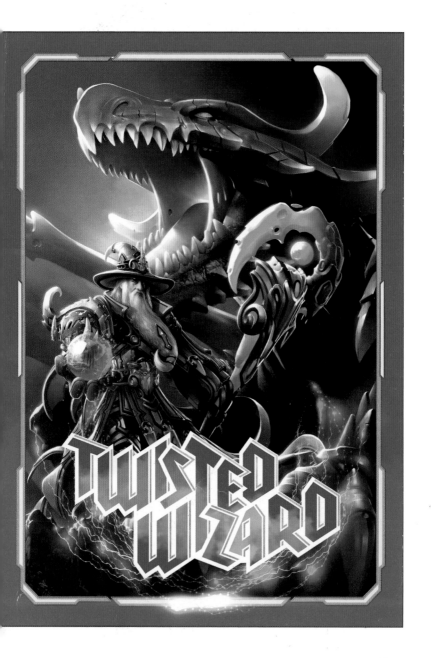

117

Each game had its own separate area on the convention floor, and each area took on the personality of the game. Some of the booths were very elaborate.

119

When you're making a movie, you have a budget—a certain amount of money you're allowed to spend. It's always a challenge to stay within the budget, and for a set like Player Expo it's easy to get carried away.

But the art department found clever ways to keep costs down. They were able to get their hands on some great stuff left over from a video-game convention that had recently wrapped up.

Some of the displays you see in the film have pieces that were used in an entirely different way in other movies.

Since Atlanta is a big movie town, there are lots of props left over from other films and television shows. If you're really paying attention, you might notice that the metal chairs in one of the booths were first used in the Hunger Games movies.

SLIIIIDE ¿

Once the convention hall was filled with colourful displays, it was time to bring in the people. Hundreds of extras were needed for the Player Expo scenes.

Most were dressed in ordinary clothes, but a number of attendees went all-out. At big conventions where people come together to celebrate movies, video games and comics, a huge number of people dress up like their favourite characters.

This is called "cosplay" and costumes can range from simple homemade outfits to professional-grade get-ups that cost thousands of dollars to create.

Some of the extras in "The Long Haul" brought their own cosplay outfits, and some were dressed up by the wardrobe department on the day of filming. The make-up department joined forces and got to show what they were really capable of.

Each booth came with its own costumed characters to represent that game. Buried under the Twisted Wizard costume was Jason Drucker's dad, who took time off from work to be an extra in the movie. He's pictured here with Rose Locke, who was in charge of casting all the extras for the film.

One of the booths at Player Expo was for a fictional game called FriendsVille, and it was manned by the author of this book. The wardrobe department's job was to make him look as dorky as possible, which clearly wasn't that easy to do.

But the biggest celebrity at Player Expo was Greg's idol, Mac Digby, who was played by Joshua Hoover. Mac is a video-game enthusiast with a gigantic YouTube following. It's Greg's dream to meet Mac —and get into one of his videos.

In the movie, Mac's such a big star that he's got not only his own stage in the convention centre but a catchphrase to rival "Zoo-Wee Mama".

A FAIR SHARE

The other big set piece in "The Long Haul" was the country fair. And, unlike Player Expo, this one was already part of the Wimpy Kid universe.

But building a giant country fair from scratch, complete with rides, food booths and livestock tents, would cost a fortune. The film-making team decided early on that the best bet would be to find a REAL country fair in the region and tag along.

Luckily, there are a handful of annual fairs in the Atlanta area, and the one held in Griffin, Georgia, fitted the bill.

The film-makers reached out to the fair organizers and asked if they could make the location a part of the movie. They agreed, under one condition: filming had to wrap at dusk every day so the gates could open to the public in the evening.

That meant the fairgrounds were a movie set during the day, and the real thing at night.

Most of the booths you see in the movie are part of the actual fair, but others were created just for the film.

When Greg and Rodrick are enjoying deep-fried butter on a stick, it's served at a stand that was created for the film. But believe it or not, in lots of places, deep-fried butter on a stick is a real thing.

129

In fact, there's a lot of weird food that's served up at your typical country fair.

When Greg and Rodrick eat fried butter in the movie, it's not a trick — it really IS fried butter. But the actors were total pros.

The fried butter was served up by character actor Ricky Muse, who plays the butter vendor.

A character actor is a performer who specializes in interesting or unusual roles. In the world of movie-making, not everyone can be the star. But there are lots of talented, quirky actors who make a living by taking small roles that have a big impact.

In fact, sometimes a character actor's performance is so memorable that it becomes everyone's favourite part of a movie.

The actors really enjoyed having the run of the fair during the day. They got to play carnival games and ride rides. Imagine having an amusement park all to yourself without having to wait in line!

Their fun wasn't limited to the daytime, either. The actors came back to enjoy the country fair at night, when it was packed with people.

One of the great things about making a film like "The Long Haul" is that the set is very family friendly.

Some of the film-makers brought their own kids to the set during the country fair shoot. And several of them made it into the film, either as background extras or as actors with spoken lines. They skipped a little school and got a taste of the movie star treatment, too.

A HAIRY SITUATION

One of the families that makes an appearance at the country fair came straight out of the pages of the book: the Beardos.

In the series, the Beardos have three sons. But for the movie, the film-makers decided to swap out the oldest boy for a girl to mix things up a little.

In the book we don't know the names of the Beardo kids. But in the movie they're Brandon, Brent and Brandi.

In "The Long Haul", Mr Beardo spends a lot of time chasing after Greg. Chris Coppola, the actor who plays Mr Beardo, modelled his performance after Bluto from the Popeye comics.

By a strange coincidence, this wasn't the first time Chris had worked with Jason Drucker. In fact, Chris has worked as Jason's acting coach on a few occasions.

By now, you're probably getting a sense that what you see on-screen isn't always the real thing. So it might not come as a big surprise that Mr Beardo's beard was also a fake. During filming, Chris Coppola was actually clean-shaven.

The beard was mesh with individual hairs strung through it, and even up close it was very convincing.

Chris wasn't the only one who got to see what it was like to have a full beard without going through the trouble of growing it.

Patrick Kinney (the original inspiration for the character Manny) had always wanted a beard, but wasn't able to grow one. On the movie set, his dream finally came true.

A ROUND TRIP

The "Long Haul" film is full of action shots, but one of the most complex sequences takes place inside the Alien Abduction ride.

If you've ever been to a carnival, you've probably ridden something like Alien Abduction. It's a circular ride that spins faster and faster, and pins its passengers to the wall.

It's a lot of fun —as long as you didn't just finish eating a couple of sticks of fried butter.

In the film, Greg and Rodrick board the ride, and are soon joined by an angry Mr Beardo, who's after Greg. The script called for Greg to flee Mr Beardo by crawling over the heads of the other passengers. Eventually, Mr Beardo rolls across Rodrick, who loses his lunch.

The director put together rough storyboards to string all the action together. The drawings are simple, but they did their job communicating exactly what was needed in each shot. On the following pages are the storyboards and the matching moments from the film.

ALIEN ENCOUNTER
SEQUENCE

CARNIE, GREG + R ENTER.
CAMERA PANS PAST CARNIE
AS THEY SETTLE AGAINST WALL

GREG LOOKS NERVOUS
CARNIE: "STAY AGIN THE WALL"

AND KEEP YER HANDS
TO YERSELVES.

140

CARNIE'S FOOT ON
BUTTON.

HIGH ANGLE AA
STARTS TO SPIN.

ROD: FEELS SICK.
G: NINTH!
OS: YOU!

MR B. FLOPS IN

STOP THE RIDE...

CARNIE HAS
HEADPHONES ON

WATCHING
DIAPER HAND

GREG STARTS TO MOVE

HIGH ANGLE SPINNING
FASTER

144

GIRL'S PIGTAILS RISE

G R

GREG STRUGGLES TO MOVE

MR B. ROLLS
OVER A KID

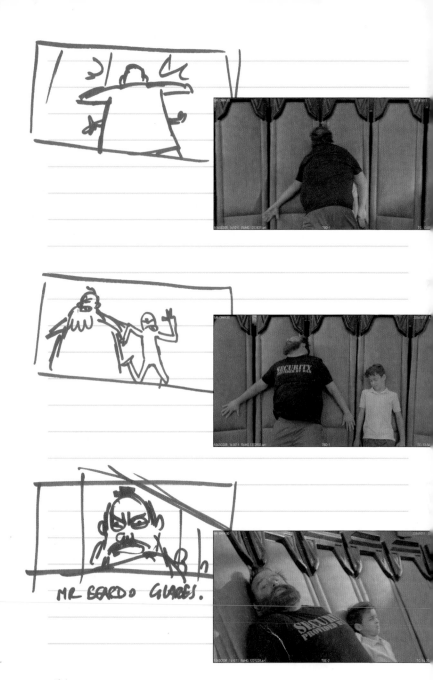

MR BEARDO GUARDS.

146

GREG TERRIFIED

TURN TO SEE
PEOPLE IN HIS WAY

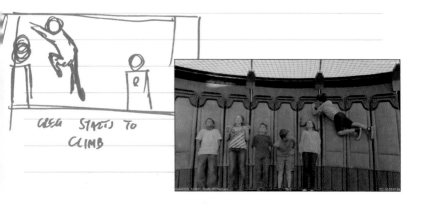

GREG STARTS TO
CLIMB

(ROD WATCHES)

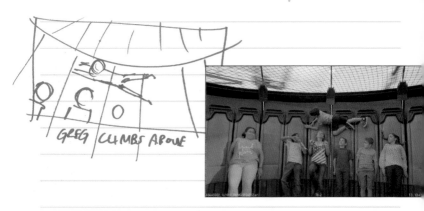

GREG CLIMBS ABOVE

B: YOU NEED TO MOVE...
R: PLEASE DON'T...

148

AMP
UP
TO

→ SLOW
MOTION

SLO-MOTION PUSH IN

SLOW MOTION VOMIT OUT

150

FULL MOTION VOMIT HITS.

CROWD HORROR

GREG HORROR.

In the film, the Alien Abduction ride looks like it's in motion the whole time. But the scene took two days to film, and that's too long to keep actors on a moving ride — no matter HOW much fun it is.

So some tricks were used to make the ride LOOK like it was spinning, even when it wasn't. Rotating lights positioned above the ride flashed across the walls to give the illusion of movement.

Giant fans positioned inside the ride gently blew the actors' hair.

When a girl's pigtails slowly rise up and stick to the wall, the film-makers used the most basic movie trick of all —fishing wire —which doesn't show up on the screen.

But when Rodrick gets sick on the ride the effect for the half-digested fried butter was created on computers long after filming ended. And the actor playing Mr Beardo was grateful for that.

PRIZE PIG

After the scenes on the Alien Abduction ride, the film-makers braced themselves for a different type of squirming — this time, of the pig variety.

The script called for Manny to win the baby pig as the grand prize in a contest for guessing the weight of a giant hog.

No one knew what to expect when the actor playing Manny was handed the pig. Would it squeal? Would it try to wriggle free? Would the actor playing Manny be too scared to hold a live animal?

The animatronic pig was on standby in case something went wrong. But when the actor playing the judge handed Manny the real live pig, the handoff went without a hitch.

The pig stayed perfectly still as Dylan cradled it in his arms. The young actor seemed comfortable holding the pig, and everyone on set was proud of him. After all, he was only three.

IN STITCHES

A good movie will draw you into the story, and you won't give a thought to how it was made. But there's a lot of work that goes into bringing it all together and creating a believable world on-screen.

Take, for instance, a sequence near the end of the movie where the Heffley family makes their final push to Meemaw's house. The scene starts at the top of a hill, where the family van has conked out.

At the bottom of the hill is Meemaw's house, where the party is winding down. The Heffleys decide to roll their van down the hill to make it to the party before it's over.

It's all part of one smooth scene, and everything takes place in one location. Or does it?

In reality, the scene was shot in three completely different locations. The hill was part of a giant duck reserve outside Atlanta, and there weren't any houses at the bottom of it — just a pond.

The digital effects team created the houses on computers and inserted them into the shot after filming wrapped.

Meemaw's house was in a neighbourhood in another part of Georgia altogether.

The flying boat wasn't really flying—it was lifted in the air by a giant crane, and the cable was digitally removed later on. And when Greg is airborne at the

wheel of the boat, he's actually on a soundstage in Atlanta, working against a green screen. Not only is the scene shot in different locations and at different times, but at certain moments even the actors are different.

When the van rolls down the hill, there are
moments when stunt doubles filled in for both
Greg and Rodrick.

Even the camera operators had substitutes for this
scene. To capture footage of Meemaw's pool from
above, a camera-carrying drone was used.

After filming was
completed, the
editor took all the
pieces and strung
them together into
one seamless scene.
Hopefully, you won't
notice the stitching that made it possible.

LET'S TAKE THIS INSIDE

Once the outdoor filming wrapped, it was time to move things indoors for the rest of the movie shoot.

There are two types of filming: on location and on a soundstage. When you're filming on location, that means you're filming in the "real world", which can be tricky because there's a lot you can't control. Just about everything that can go wrong often does.

But on a soundstage the movie's world is completely in the director's control.

A typical soundstage is a giant building that's big enough to hold a jumbo jet. Since it's indoors, there's no need to worry about the weather.

In fact, if you want, you can make your OWN weather.

Most of today's movies with lots of big special effects are filmed on soundstages, because when you're spending all that money you can't worry about things you can't control. If you've ever seen a movie that's about superheroes or one that's set in a galaxy far, far away, chances are a lot of it was actually filmed indoors on a soundstage.

Since "The Long Haul" was about a road trip, there weren't that many scenes that were shot on a soundstage. But there were a few exceptions.

The motels you see in the film are real-life buildings, but their rooms were re-created on the soundstage, down to the last detail.

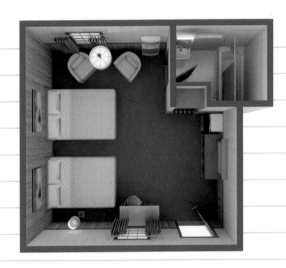

Being on a soundstage can be a strange experience. Most of the space looks like a dark, empty warehouse. But the areas for filming look like little slices of the real world.

The actors quickly get used to their unusual surroundings.

Not every soundstage set is meant to look like an indoor environment. Sometimes the film-makers can't get a shot they wanted on location, so they'll re-create the scene on a soundstage and pick up filming again later on. This was the case with an outdoor pool at the motel where the Heffleys stay on their first night. Here's what the original outdoor set looked like:

The pool wasn't actually real — it was built from scratch just for the movie. Even the breeze-block walls are fake. They were made out of lightweight foam and painted to look like they'd seen better days.

Weeks after the outdoor shoot, the fake pool scene was brought on to the soundstage and reassembled indoors. In the movie, there are moments that were filmed outdoors on location, and moments that were filmed inside. When you're watching the film, see if you can tell the difference.

One of the best things about a soundstage is how much room there is inside.

There's a scene early in the movie where Greg goes down a big slide at Corny's. The scene is filmed

from inside the slide, and the camera follows Greg as he twists and turns his way down into the ball pit.

At Corny's restaurant, there wasn't room for a giant slide. So a slide was assembled on the soundstage, where space isn't an issue.

Almost all the sets on the soundstage were re-creations of real-life settings. But one of the sets didn't have a real-life version at all.

Greg's bedroom only existed on the soundstage. In the first three films, Greg had the same room. But since the new movie had a different actor playing Greg, giving him a new bedroom felt like the right thing to do.

THE IMITATION GAME

Movie-making's been around a long time — over 125 years. There have been lots of famous directors throughout film-making history, and one of the most famous of them all was Alfred Hitchcock.

Hitchcock was nicknamed the "Master of Suspense", and for good reason. He made films that kept moviegoers on the edge of their seats. In fact, some of his movies were downright terrifying.

Hitchcock's work has had a huge influence on thousands of directors who came after him. And one of those directors was David Bowers, who grew up watching Hitchcock's films.

In film-making, when one director pays tribute to another director's style, it's called an "homage". It's the ultimate sign of respect from one artist to another.

In "The Long Haul", there are two scenes where David mimics Hitchcock's style. One of the scenes is where seagulls attack the Heffleys' van. Hitchcock directed a movie called "The Birds", in which people in a California town are terrorized by flocks of — you guessed it — birds. Hitchcock's

most famous movie was called "Psycho", and it's definitely not for kids — or for the faint of heart.

The most memorable scene in the movie takes place in a motel bathroom. Specifically, in a shower.

David created a comical version of the film's "shower scene" to give adults who are familiar with Hitchcock's terrifying masterpiece a good chuckle — and to give kids a good scare.

GOING GREEN

When it comes to special effects, one of the most commonly used tricks is shooting in front of a green screen. Actors perform in front of a large piece of green cloth, which is swapped out for a different background in post-production.

In the beginning of all four Wimpy Kid movies, Greg talks directly to the audience while holding his diar— uh, make that journal.

The actor delivers his lines in front of a green screen, which is replaced by a drawing of Greg's bedroom later on.

There were other parts of the movie where a green screen was needed. Most of these images require no explanation, but you'll have to see the film to make sense of that last one.

ON THE ROAD AGAIN

In "The Long Haul", there are lots of scenes that take place inside the minivan. But shooting a scene inside a moving car with five actors and a pig is no easy task, so the film-makers had to figure out a different way to make it work.

They came up with an interesting solution. First, a team travelled around Atlanta with a truck that had nine cameras pointed in all different directions. The cameras captured everything surrounding the truck —even the sky above.

Next, a special set was built on the soundstage with large monitors surrounding the buck car. The footage captured weeks before was then played back on the big screens.

This gives the illusion that the van is moving, and the effect is really convincing.

Even when the van isn't moving — such as the scene where the Heffleys get lost in the woods — it's very hard to tell that the shots behind the van aren't real.

It took about a week to shoot all the scenes inside the van. The actors had to re-create their whole experience of filming, wearing the same

clothes they wore throughout the movie — and got gooped up all over again.

But it wasn't mud and cinnamon rolls all the time. If it looks like the actors were having a blast singing along to a Spice Girls song, it's because they really were.

By the time things wrapped up, the cast and crew had been through a lot together. "The Long Haul" is about how the fictional Heffley family comes together by taking a road trip. But, in making the movie, the actors and everyone who helped had bonded as well.

With filming finished, everyone went their separate ways. The actors went home, and the director and producers went back to the film studio to finish the last big stage of the movie-making process — post-production.

CUT!

The post-production phase is when all the editing, special effects, animation and music get done. It's also when the director and editor start making tough decisions about what moments from the film to keep and what to leave out.

There are lots of reasons for cutting footage from a movie. Sometimes a scene is too long and needs to be trimmed. Sometimes a moment is cut because it's getting in the way of the story. And sometimes something that seemed like a good idea at the time just doesn't work on-screen.

It's always hard to let go of footage, because it took so much work to create it in the first place.

Here are a few moments that got filmed, but for one reason or another didn't make the cut.

The Corny's scene used to be a lot longer than it is in the final version of the film. In one part, Greg's dad gets his tie snipped off and put up on the Wall of Shame, just like it happens in Book 7, "The Third Wheel".

Another Corny's moment that was cut from the film is when Greg awkwardly makes eye contact with a guy at the urinal.

Lots of other moments were trimmed from the movie during editing, too. But, just like the stiff piece of underwear Greg finds along the side of the road, there are some things that just need to be tossed out. Each cut is done in the hopes of making the movie better.

PAGE TO SCREEN

Even though some moments from the book got cut from the film, there were plenty of others that made the movie. Here are some Wimpy Kid illustrations and their real-life equivalents.

SNUFFLE
GRUNT

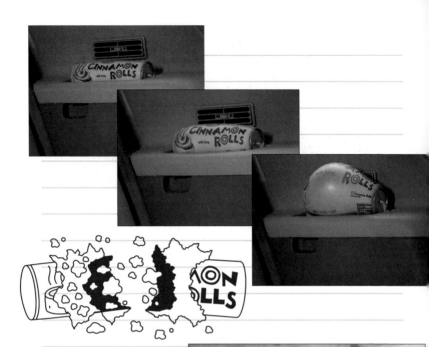

GOING THROUGH THE MOTIONS

While the editing team was piecing the film together, a separate group was working on animating Greg's journal illustrations. Each drawing starts off as a pencil sketch on paper, like this one:

The drawings are scanned into a computer, and the artists trace over them in clean, smooth lines. For each character, the animators create a "skeleton", which helps guide how the character moves. The skeleton isn't visible to the audience, but it's an essential tool for the artists to create motion.

The animators bring the drawings to life by creating frame-by-frame sequences of the action. A technique called "onion skinning" helps the artists keep track of what the animation looks like before and after the current frame.

In the images below, the red areas show what happened before, and the green areas show what will happen next.

FACING THE MUSIC

After the final changes have been made to the film, it's time to add the "score". The score is the music that sets the mood for the movie and helps the audience know how to feel during a scene. The music can be upbeat for a happy scene and tense for a scary one.

To record the score, a full orchestra, complete with drums and electric guitars, performs in front of the screen while the movie plays. The conductor helps the orchestra match the music with what's happening in the film.

Music is a very important part of a movie, but, unless you're really paying close attention, you won't always notice it. But sometimes the score is front and centre.

For the motel shower scene, the iconic violin screeching from the movie "Psycho" was used to add tension to the scene.

Getting the score finished is the last major step in the movie-making process. And once it's finished it's time to bring it out into the world.

GETTING THE WORD OUT

Before a film is completely finished, the marketing department starts telling people that the movie is coming. This step is a huge part of the success of a motion picture, because if the public doesn't know that a film is in cinemas, even if it's great, it won't do well.

One of the most important tools the marketing department has is the "trailer". A trailer is a short clip that gives the public a sense of what to expect in a film. Creating a good trailer is an art form. You want to show enough of the good parts of the movie to get people excited—but not TOO much, or they won't need to see the film.

SPLASH!

OH, COME ON!

But the trailer is just one tool the marketing department has to reach filmgoers. The average person has to hear about a movie multiple times for it to really sink in that the movie is coming out.

That makes marketing very expensive. Sometimes a movie studio will spend just as much money marketing a movie as it does MAKING the film. And the bigger the movie, the more money that goes into marketing.

The marketing department creates giant billboards, commercials on television, ads on buses and in magazines, social media posts, and displays in cinemas to make sure people know about the film.

Here are a handful of the concepts that the marketing team put together to spread the word about "The Long Haul".

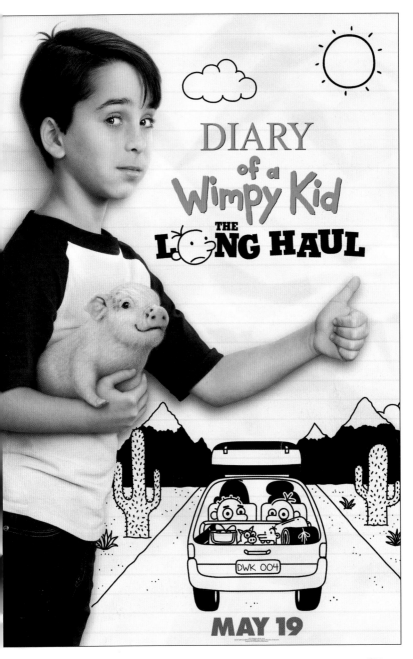

195

196

END OF THE ROAD?

Making "The Long Haul" was an epic experience for everyone involved. It was hard work, but by the end the actors, the film-makers and everyone else who participated grew from the journey.

For the Kinney family, the movie created a chance to reconnect. These days, they live in different parts of the country, but filming brought them together in Atlanta.

Who knows what's next for the Heffley family? Will they be in more films, or have they reached the end of the road? That's up to audiences to decide. But, whatever the case, it's been an amazing trip so far.

CREDITS

FOX 2000 PICTURES Presents

A COLOR FORCE Production

"DIARY OF A WIMPY KID: THE LONG HAUL"

JASON DRUCKER
ALICIA SILVERSTONE
TOM EVERETT SCOTT
CHARLIE WRIGHT
OWEN ASZTALOS

Costume Designer
MARY CLAIRE HANNAN

Music Supervisor
JULIA MICHELS

Music by
EDWARD SHEARMUR

Film Editor
TROY TAKAKI, ACE

Production Designer
AARON OSBORNE

Director of Photography
ANTHONY B. RICHMOND, ASC/BSC

Executive Producers
JEFF KINNEY
TIMOTHY M. BOURNE
DAVID BOWERS

Produced by
NINA JACOBSON, P.G.A.
BRAD SIMPSON, P.G.A.

Based upon the book by
JEFF KINNEY

Screenplay by
JEFF KINNEY and DAVID BOWERS

Directed by
DAVID BOWERS

FOX 2000 PICTURES PRESENTS A COLOR FORCE PRODUCTION "DIARY OF A WIMPY KID: THE LONG HAUL"
ON DRUCKER   ALICIA SILVERSTONE   TOM EVERETT SCOTT   CHARLIE WRIGHT   OWEN ASZTALOS   COSTUME DESIGNER MARY CLAIRE HANNAN
MUSIC SUPERVISOR JULIA MICHELS   MUSIC BY EDWARD SHEARMUR   FILM EDITOR TROY TAKAKI, ACE   PRODUCTION DESIGNER AARON OSBORNE
DIRECTOR OF PHOTOGRAPHY ANTHONY B. RICHMOND, ASC/BSC   EXECUTIVE PRODUCERS JEFF KINNEY   TIMOTHY M. BOURNE   DAVID BOWERS
PRODUCED BY NINA JACOBSON, p.g.a.   BRAD SIMPSON, p.g.a.   BASED UPON THE BOOK BY JEFF KINNEY   SCREENPLAY BY JEFF KINNEY AND DAVID BOWERS
DIRECTED BY DAVID BOWERS

ACKNOWLEDGEMENTS

Thanks to everyone who helped me put this book together. Thanks to Nina Jacobson and Brad Simpson for being my partners on the Wimpy Kid films. Thanks to David Bowers for directing **The Long Haul,** for your insights into film-making, and for the bonus photos and storyboards. Thanks to Dan McFadden for the fantastic unit photography and for helping kids get a behind-the-scenes look at the movie-making process. Thanks to Aaron Osborne for bringing the Wimpy Kid universe to life with so much enthusiasm and joy. Thanks to Ken Terry for getting me the shots I needed during your crunch time. And thanks to Rose Locke for being so much fun.

Thanks to everyone at Fox, especially Elizabeth Gabler and Greg Moridian, for being champions of these books. Thanks to Nick D'Angelo for helping get this movie off the ground. Thanks to the production team, art department and to all the graphic artists, set designers and set decorators whose work I've displayed in this book. Thanks to Tony O'Dell for returning to the Wimpy Kid movies as an acting coach and for being a good friend. Thanks to Max Graenitz and your team for doing such a great job of animating the characters. Thanks to Nicole Spiegel for all your help in pushing this project forward!

Thanks to Jason Drucker and the entire cast for being such a big part of the Wimpy world.

Thanks to all the great folks at Abrams for pulling off the impossible and getting this book out on time, especially Charlie Kochman, Samantha Hoback, Amy Vreeland, Masha Gunic, Chad W. Beckerman, Veronica Wasserman and Alison Gervais.

Thanks to my agent, Sylvie Rabineau, for being a guiding force and a great friend. Thanks to my lawyers, Paul Sennott and Keith Fleer, for all your help over the years.